PILLAR BOX RED

in association with

© 2025. Published by Pillar Box Red Publishing Limited under licence from Kelsey Media.
Pillar Box Red Publishing Limited, 25 Herbert Place, Dublin, D02 AY86
info@pillarboxredpublishing.co.uk

Printed in Romania.

This publication has no connection with Rangers Football Club, or any of the clubs featured, or with any organisation/s or individual/s connected in any way whatsoever with Rangers Football Club, or any of the clubs, featured.

Any quotes within this publication which are attributed to anyone connected to Rangers Football Club, or any of the clubs featured, have been sourced from other publications, or from the internet and, as such, are a matter of public record.

Whilst every effort has been made to ensure the accuracy of information within this publication, the publisher shall have no liability to any person or entity with respect to any inaccuracy, misleading information, loss or damage caused directly or indirectly by information within this book.

The views expressed are solely those of the author and do not reflect the opinions of Pillar Box Red Publishing Limited or Kelsey Media. All rights reserved.

ISBN: 978-1-917522-11-3

Images © Shutterstock & Alamy

RANGERS ANNUAL 2026

Witten by Iain Williamson
Designed by Chris Dalrymple

AN INDEPENDENT PRODUCTION

CONTENTS

- **8** SEASON REVIEW
- **18** THE FOUR BEARS
- **20** IBROX 1899-2024: PART 1
- **22** NEW MANAGER: RUSSELL MARTIN
- **23** NEW BOSS: LEANNE CRICHTON
- **24** INTERNATIONAL BROTHERS
- **25** COLOURING IN
- **26** EUROPEAN NIGHTS
- **28** RANGERS WOMEN SEASON REVIEW
- **29** CUP DOUBLE AT THE DOUBLE
- **30** RANGERS WOMEN KATIE & LAURA
- **31** CHASING THE TITLE DREAM
- **32** IBROX 1899-2024: PART 2
- **34** WORD SEARCH
- **35** SPOT THE DIFFERENCE

- **36** LEGEND: DAVIE COOPER
- **38** ACADEMY
- **40** AWARDS NIGHT
- **42** IBROX 1899-2024: PART 3
- **44** NEW PLAYER PROFILES
- **46** SPOT THE BALL AND ANAGRAMS
- **47** WHO ARE SAN FRANCISCO 49ERS
- **48** THE CAPTAIN: NICOLA DOCHERTY
- **50** IBROX 1899-2024: PART 4
- **52** A LOOK BACK IN TIME
- **54** SQUAD PROFILES & NEW SIGNINGS
- **58** IBROX 1899-2024: PART 5
- **60** ANSWERS
- **62** CLUB HONOURS

SEASON REVIEW

After further turmoil both on and off the pitch, 2024/25 was largely another season to forget for Rangers' loyal supporters as the team failed to add any further trophies to the famous Glasgow club's impressive list of honours.

The season started in disarray with a temporary residence at Hampden for the first month of the season after planned summer improvements at Ibrox were delayed.

A sparkling Europa League adventure was the clear highlight in an inconsistent season.

With the league title already out of reach, an embarrassing home defeat to Queens Park in the Scottish Cup ultimately cost manager Philippe Clement his job in February – the 4th managerial departure in as many years.

Ibrox legend and former skipper Barry Ferguson was brought in on an interim basis to steady the ship but an unprecedented slump in home form continued and, despite a couple of good wins over their old foes, Rangers were unable to prevent city rivals Celtic claiming a record-equalling 55th title.

AUGUST 2024

MEGA MOMENT

After a stuttering start to the season, an unanswered six-goal blitz against Ross County at Hampden provided a much-needed boost to Rangers' morale as they ended the first month unbeaten in domestic competitions.

STAR MAN

Cyriel Dessers was one of Rangers' leading marksmen in the previous campaign and he got his second season off to a flying start with five goals in August, including a late equalizer against displaced Dynamo Kyiv in Poland and a brace against Ross County.

With Ibrox unavailable, Rangers had to relocate to Hampden Park for the entire month of August. Three wins at their temporary home and two creditable away draws was a reasonable start but defeat at the national stadium against Ukrainian champions Kyiv brought disappointment and another early Champions League exit.

DATE	COMP	HOME	RESULT	AWAY
03/08	SPL	Hearts	0-0	Rangers
06/08	UCL	Dynamo Kyiv	1-1	Rangers
10/08	SPL	Rangers	2-1	Motherwell
13/08	UCL	Rangers	0-2	Dynamo Kyiv
17/08	SLC	Rangers	2-0	St Johnstone
24/08	SPL	Rangers	6-0	Ross County

SEPTEMBER 2024

The only blemish on Rangers' record in September was a significant one. Defeat in the first Old Firm game of the year allowed Celtic to open up an early 5-point gap and left manager Philippe Clement win-less against his team's greatest rivals in five attempts. Goals from Bajrami and McCausland got their Europa League campaign off to a good start though and a solid defence delivered four clean sheets throughout the rest of the month.

MEGA MOMENT

Despite four wins in September, the best news of the month was Rangers return to Ibrox in time for the Dundee game and the opening of the full ground for the visit of Hibs at the end of the month. The Copland Road stand now features improved accessible facilities and increased capacity.

STAR MAN

Welsh attacker Tom Lawrence showed the kind of form which would earn him a recall to his national team with only-goal-of-the-game winners at Tannadice and at home to Hibs. He would add European goals in October before succumbing to long-term injury in early November.

DATE	COMP	HOME	RESULT	AWAY
01/09	SPL	Celtic	3-0	Rangers
15/09	SPL	Dundee United	0-1	Rangers
21/09	SPL	Rangers	3-0	Dundee
26/09	SPL	Malmo	0-2	Rangers
29/09	SPL	Rangers	1-0	Hibernian

OCTOBER 2024

The defeat at Pittodrie was Rangers' third of the month and left them nine points behind the unbeaten Dons and joint-leaders Celtic. Some insipid displays and fan discontent at the lack of demonstrable progress in Clement's second season significantly increased the pressure on the beleaguered Belgian.

STAR MAN

On-loan from VfL Wolfsburg, winger Vaclav Cerny played a big part in all three Rangers victories this month. The Czech struck five times in October, including both goals against St Johnstone, another brace against FCSB and the winner at home to St Mirren.

MEGA MOMENT

After abject defeat at Kilmarnock the previous week, a rousing performance against Romanian's FCSB was a much-needed boost for everyone at Ibrox. The returning Nico Raskin was described as "a man possessed" by BBC pundit Neil McCann, while substitute Hamza Igamane notched his first Rangers goal in the second half.

DATE	COMP	HOME	RESULT	AWAY
03/10	UEL	Rangers	1-4	Olympique Lyonnais
06/10	SPL	Rangers	2-0	St Johnstone
20/10	SPL	Kilmarnock	1-0	Rangers
24/10	UEL	Rangers	4-0	FCSB
27/10	SPL	Rangers	2-1	St Mirren
30/10	SPL	Aberdeen	2-1	Rangers

NOVEMBER 2024

After a challenging run in October, a second half turnaround against Motherwell at Hampden sent Rangers to the Premier Sports Cup final and set up an unbeaten month in November.

The Light Blues' domestic form remained unconvincing but two good away performances in the Europa League were obvious highlights.

STAR MAN

After eight games without a goal, Cyriel Dessers made the difference in the first three games in November. He was "The Equalizer" in cup games against Motherwell and Olympiakos before notching the only goal of the game in the league match at Ibrox against Hearts.

MEGA MOMENT

Philippe Clement described the performance in Nice as "close to perfection" as Hamza Igamane showcased his potential with two goals and Vaclav Cerny continued his hot form with 5 goal involvements in his last 3 European games (3 goals / 2 assists).

DATE	COMP	HOME	RESULT	AWAY
03/11	SLC SF	Motherwell	1-2	Rangers
07/11	UEL	Olympiakos	1-1	Rangers
10/11	SPL	Rangers	1-0	Heart of Midlothian
23/11	SPL	Rangers	1-1	Dundee United
28/11	UEL	Nice	1-4	Rangers

DECEMBER 2024

Nine points from three SPFL games and ten goals without reply was a great start to a very busy month. A raucous Ibrox game against Spurs and a valiant effort against Celtic at Hampden stirred the emotions before cup final penalty shoot-out heart-break burst Rangers' bubble.

Lucky Rangers fans will have found the Rangers Annual 2025 in their Xmas stockings, but then had little festive cheer after that as the team's poor domestic away form saw more points dropped by the end of the year.

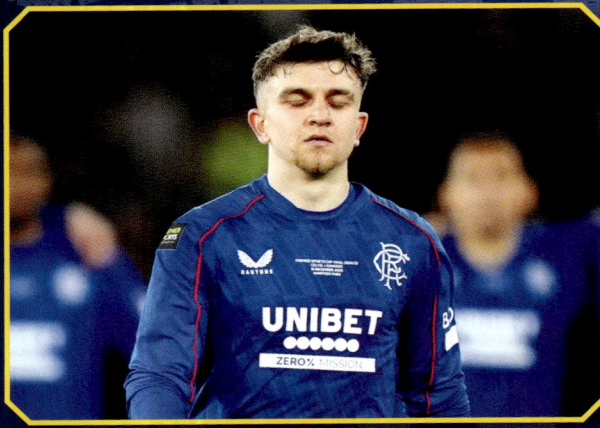

STAR MAN

Danilo and Hamza Igamane both have good claims after their goal-scoring exploits, but the form of Ianis Hagi on his return to the first team after a loan spell in Spain and exile to the B team also made a big impact.

MEGA MOMENT

Danilo's very late equalizer against Celtic capped an incredible Rangers effort in the Premier Sports Cup final. Six yellow cards for the team after the Brazilian's dramatic goal demonstrated the level of fight and commitment shown in a final that was ultimately decided by Schmeichel's penalty save from Ridvan Yilmaz.

DATE	COMP	HOME	RESULT	AWAY
01/12	SPL	St Johnstone	0-1	Rangers
04/12	SPL	Rangers	6-0	Kilmarnock
08/12	SPL	Ross County	0-3	Rangers
12/12	UEL	Rangers	1-1	Tottenham Hotspur
15/12	SLC Final	Celtic	3-3 AET (5-4 pens)	Rangers
21/12	SPL	Rangers	1-0	Dundee
26/12	SPL	St Mirren	2-1	Rangers
29/12	SPL	Motherwell	2-2	Rangers

JANUARY 2025

A home win over Celtic was a great start to the year. Away from Ibrox, consecutive draws at Hibs and Dundee continued a poor run of form on the road, although Rangers still bagged 14 league points in January and progressed in the Scottish Cup. An exciting but ultimately heart-breaking performance at Old Trafford was a highlight for travelling supporters and a last-matchday win over Belgian's USG earned Rangers an automatic place in the knockout stages of the revamped Europa League.

STAR MAN

Hamza Igamane won the Premiership Player of the Month for January after a strong showing. The highlight was a "perfect" hat-trick at Easter Road – scoring with both his left and right feet either side of a headed goal. The young Moroccan also netted against St Johnstone and Aberdeen.

MEGA MOMENT

Rangers' first goal of 2025 arrived after only 7 minutes of the New Year derby. Strong work from Nicolas Raskin set up Ianis Hagi for a sweet and low 25-yard finish to open the scoring. A rampant Rangers team would go on to clinch Philippe Clement's first (and last) Old Firm victory by three goals to nil.

DATE	COMP	HOME	RESULT	AWAY
02/01	SPL	Rangers	3-0	Celtic
05/01	SPL	Hibernian	3-3	Rangers
09/01	SPL	Dundee	1-1	Rangers
12/01	SPL	Rangers	3-1	St Johnstone
15/01	SPL	Rangers	3-0	Aberdeen
19/01	SC	Rangers	5-0	Fraserburgh
23/01	UEL	Manchester United	2-1	Rangers
26/01	SPL	Dundee United	1-3	Rangers
30/01	UEL	Rangers	2-1	Union Saint-Gilloise

FEBRUARY 2025

The 4-0 home win over Ross County continued Rangers' season-long unbeaten run at Ibrox in Scottish fixtures, but shockingly, it would be the club's last home win for three months.

The subsequent defeat by Queen's Park was the first time Rangers has ever been knocked out of the Scottish Cup at home by lower-league opposition and ended any hopes of domestic honours for the season.

A second consecutive home defeat, this time to St Mirren, brought an end to Philippe Clement's reign as Rangers' manager, with former captain Barry Ferguson brought in to replace him on an interim basis.

STAR MAN

No Rangers player truly excelled during a disastrous month for the club. Vaclav Cerny was the only Rangers player to score at Tynecastle, where Jamie McCart's own goal double proved decisive, and the Czech also started the crucial face-saving fightback at Rugby Park with the first Rangers' goal of the Ferguson era.

MEGA MOMENT

Being appointed Rangers manager was a dream come true for Barry Ferguson, but his tenure got off to a nightmare start as his team went 2-0 down at Kilmarnock within 14 minutes. An early defensive substitution, a Cerny goal and a half-time rollicking got Rangers back on track before a Dessers double and a late Bajrami strike averted further embarrassment.

DATE	COMP	HOME	RESULT	AWAY
02/02	SPL	Rangers	4-0	Ross County
09/02	SC	Rangers	0-1	Queen's Park
16/02	SPL	Heart of Midlothian	1-3	Rangers
22/02	SPL	Rangers	0-2	St Mirren
26/02	SPL	Kilmarnock	2-4	Rangers

MARCH 2025

Rangers' run of consecutive home defeats continued after an abject display against Motherwell, although the loss to José Mourinho's Fenerbahçe was mitigated by the aggregate score and a penalty shoot-out win.

Conversely, the Ibrox club's away form yielded three dramatic wins. These included a stunning triumph in Turkey, a second consecutive win over Glaswegian rivals Celtic and a stoppage-time winner at Dens Park from Cyriel Dessers on his 100th appearance for the club, capping another fine fight-back from an early 2-0 deficit.

STAR MAN

Diminutive Belgian midfielder Nico Raskin had a memorable month. At Celtic Park, he used his head to flick in a corner for the first goal and then rose to nod an assist for Mo Diomande to double Rangers' advantage.

The next week, his good form was rewarded with a first cap for his country, followed a few days later by a first international start in a man-of-the-match performance against Ukraine.

MEGA MOMENT

After barely controlling Jack Butland's long-hoof, a thumping long-range finish by Hamza Igamane clinched a dramatic victory at Parkhead after Barry Ferguson's side's two-goal advantage had been pegged back by Celtic.

DATE	COMP	HOME	RESULT	AWAY
01/03	SPL	Rangers	1-2	Motherwell
06/03	UEL	Fenerbahçe	1-3	Rangers
13/03	UEL	Rangers	0-2 (Pens 3-2)	Fenerbahçe
16/03	SPL	Celtic	2-3	Rangers
29/03	SPL	Dundee	3-4	Rangers

APRIL 2025

With new manager Ferguson still to taste victory at Ibrox, the only winning performance for Rangers' supporters to cheer in April came from ex-pat super-fan Drew McIntyre at Wrestlemania 41 in Las Vegas. The loss against Hibs was a record-breaking fifth consecutive home defeat for the Ibrox side and a swashbuckling European campaign came to an end with defeat in Bilbao, despite a courageous effort.

STAR MAN

Liam Kelly regained the goalkeeper's gloves after Jack Butland's error against Hibs. He became an instant hero with a late penalty save which preserved a draw for 10-man Rangers against Bilbao in the first leg of the Europa League quarter final tie at Ibrox.

MEGA MOMENT

At Pittodrie, Ferguson's side started slowly and faced a 2-0 deficit for the 6th time under his management. Even after Ross McCausland's dismissal, Rangers again showed resilience to battle back and salvage a point with a very late strike from Ianis Hagi.

DATE	COMP	HOME	RESULT	AWAY
05/04	SPL	Rangers	0-2	Hibernian
10/04	UEL	Rangers	0-0	Athletic Club Bilbao
13/04	SPL	Aberdeen	2-2	Rangers
17/04	UEL	Athletic Club Bilbao	2-0	Rangers
26/04	SPL	St Mirren	2-2	Rangers

MAY 2025

To everyone's relief, a thumping 4-0 win over Aberdeen ended Rangers and Barry Ferguson's win-less run at Ibrox. They followed that up with another home win over Dundee United in a month book-ended by draws with Celtic and Hibs, the latter partly due to a 'ball-not-over-the-line' controversy that denied Nico Raskin a goal.

Ferguson's brief tenure as a manager ended with a record of six wins from 15 games, having steered the club through a difficult spell in a challenging season.

STAR MAN

Nicolas Raskin inspired Rangers' four-goal romp over Aberdeen with two assists. Before the season ended, he added two goals and a further assist to round off a break-through season where he claimed Player of the Year honours and his first Belgian caps.

MEGA MOMENT

Cyriel Dessers' 73rd minute penalty against Dundee United was his 28th goal of the season and the 50th of his Rangers career. The following week, he took his Premiership tally to 19 at Easter Road to end the season as the league's top-scorer.

DATE	COMP	HOME	RESULT	AWAY
04/05	SPL	Rangers	1-1	Celtic
11/05	SPL	Rangers	4-0	Aberdeen
14/05	SPL	Rangers	3-1	Dundee United
17/05	SPL	Hibernian	2-2	Rangers

THE FOUR BEARS

After the end of Graeme Murty's second interim spell in 2018, the role of Rangers manager had been filled by 2 Northern Irishmen, 2 Englishmen, a Dutchman and a Belgian. In February 2025, the honour passed back to a Scotsman when Barry Ferguson stepped in to become the first Scottish-born ex-Rangers captain to manage the club since John Greig CBE (1978-1983).

With the official title of Head Coach, Ferguson's coaching staff included the retention of Belgian-Moroccan coach Issame Charai and was completed by the addition of three other returning Ibrox legends; Neil McCann, Billy Dodds and Hall of Fame goalkeeper Allan McGregor.

BARRY FERGUSON

As a manager, Ferguson helped Kelty Hearts into the SPFL but failed to achieve significant success as a boss at Blackpool, Clyde and Alloa, leaving the Clackmannanshire club in 2022. As a Rangers player, he was appointed club captain at the age of 22 and went on to win 15 major honours over two spells in Royal Blue. He is considered the finest home-grown midfield talent in the club's recent history.

NEIL McCANN

As a player, McCann was a key part of two Rangers treble wins. Despite brief managerial and coaching stints at Dunfermline, Dundee and Inverness, McCann is best known as a knowledgeable and forthright pundit on TV.

BILLY DODDS

Like the others, Dodds achieved success as a player at Ibrox and internationally with Scotland. He worked with McCann at Inverness CT and eventually succeeded him as manager there. An outspoken critic of Clement's Rangers while on TV, he accepted the offer to put his opinions into practice as part of Ferguson's coaching staff.

ALLAN McGREGOR

A serial winner over two spells in Govan, the iconic goalie is revered by fans as one of the most important characters to serve the club this century. His unexpected return as goalkeeping coach was very welcome.

THE FOUR AS TEAM MATES

According to Rangers historians, the four coaches only briefly appeared together as Rangers players on one occasion. Ferguson, McCann and Dodds were regulars in the 2001/02 season but McGregor was just a young back-up for Stefan Klos then. He shared a pitch with the other three for only 16 minutes after coming on as a substitute in a Scottish Cup quarter-final at Forfar Athletic on Sunday 24th February 2002.

All four were in the matchday squad for the 2002 League Cup final win but while McCann and Dodds substituted on to join captain Ferguson, McGregor remained on the bench.

SUMMARY

In his 84 days in charge, Ferguson led the club to 6 wins, 5 draws and 4 defeats from 15 games; a win percentage of 40%.

An attempt to inject passion, belief and old-school Rangers' values yielded improved away form, including a win at Celtic Park, and a brave run to the Europa League quarter-finals but a squad badly in need of a refresh was unable to rise to the challenge at home and Ferguson's reign will likely be defined by the continuation of a record-breaking streak of seven Ibrox games without a victory.

IBROX STADIUM: 1899-2024
PART 1: IBROX 125

Rangers celebrated Ibrox Stadium's 125th birthday in December 2024.

The 19th century building, then known as Ibrox Park, was formally opened with a 3-1 victory over Hearts on 31st December 1899.

The reigning monarch at that time was Queen Victoria and Britain was still engaged in the Second Boer War. Ibrox pre-dates the Kelvin Hall and many other Glasgow landmarks. Although many of its contemporaries have been torn down, the grand old Govan ground has undergone many changes but is still one of the finest and most recognisable football arenas in the country.

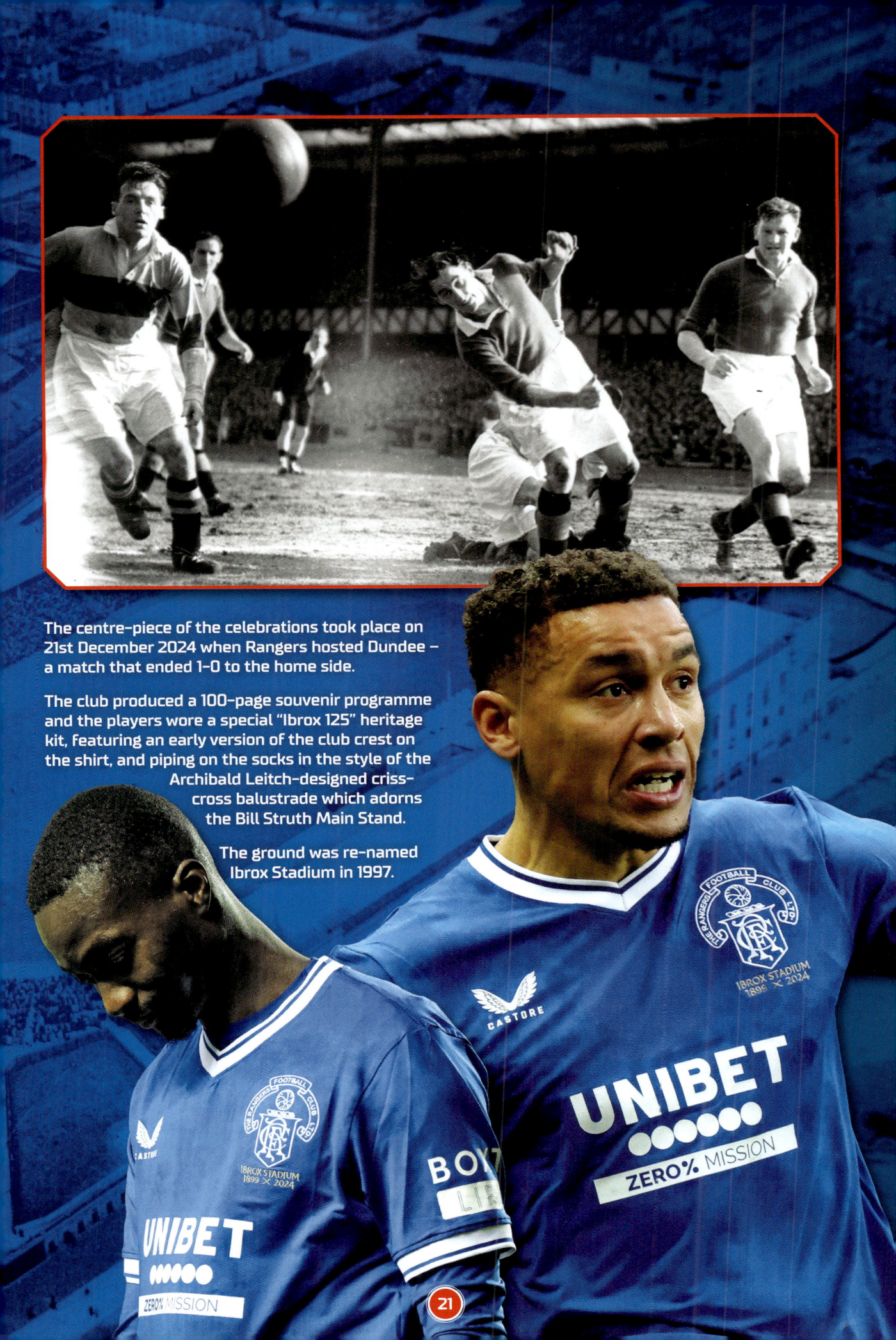

The centre-piece of the celebrations took place on 21st December 2024 when Rangers hosted Dundee – a match that ended 1-0 to the home side.

The club produced a 100-page souvenir programme and the players wore a special "Ibrox 125" heritage kit, featuring an early version of the club crest on the shirt, and piping on the socks in the style of the Archibald Leitch-designed criss-cross balustrade which adorns the Bill Struth Main Stand.

The ground was re-named Ibrox Stadium in 1997.

RUSSELL MARTIN – DID YOU KNOW?

Russell was born in Brighton, East Sussex on 4th January 1986.

On that day, 'West End Girls' by The Pet Shop Boys was the UK Number One.

At Ibrox, Jock Wallace's Rangers beat Dundee 5-0 on a snowy day in Govan in front of 13,954 fans.

Rangers' scorers were Ally McCoist (3), Bobby Williamson and Robert Fleck.

Although born in England, Russell qualified to play for Scotland through his father, Dean.

Between 2011 and 2017, he was capped 29 times under Craig Levein and then Gordon Strachan.

He made his debut against Wales in a friendly tournament staged in Dublin in May 2011. Russell replaced Stephen Crainey in the 81st minute, joining Allan McGregor, Kenny Miller and Steven Naismith on the pitch.

His final appearance was a World Cup Qualifier at home to Slovenia in March 2017. Scotland won 1-0 with a Martin goal – but it was Chris Martin (of Derby County not Coldplay).

Russell never scored for Scotland and did not appear in any major finals.

In 2024, Russell was awarded an honorary degree from the University of Brighton for his charitable work.

Russell is the Founder and Chair of the Russell Martin Foundation; a registered charity that works to impact positively upon the lives of children, young people and adults through football, education, health and improvement.

Russell was briefly a player for Rangers after coming in on loan from Norwich City in January 2018.

In all, Russell made 17 appearances for the club, scoring once – against Hearts on 24th February 2018 with a close-range poke in the 88th minute to seal a 2-0 win.

Although 2017/18 was a largely forgettable season for the Ibrox club, Russell's last game in light blue was the memorable 5-5 draw against Hibs at Easter Road. Among Russell's team-mates that day was James Tavernier.

MEET THE NEW BOSS: LEANNE CRICHTON

Rangers turned to one of the most respected names in Scottish Women's football to replace Jo Potter as manager.

Leanne Crichton enjoyed a stellar career as a player, winning 72 Scotland caps and a drawer full of medals from three stints at Glasgow City and other clubs in Scotland and England. Leanne finally hung up her boots in 2023 and, as well as coaching, she subsequently excelled as a knowledgeable and authoritative pundit on BBC Scotland's coverage of the women's game.

Her first coaching experience came as player/coach with Motherwell and she went on to gain her UEFA Pro License and return to Glasgow City in 2024 as assistant to Leanne Ross.

The 37-year-old took up her first Head Coach role in August 2025 when she signed a 3-year contract at Ibrox.

CLUB PLAYER

The second of Leanne's three spells with Glasgow City (2012-2014) was the most successful. In 2012, City achieved a domestic clean sweep of honours, including an unbeaten league campaign.

A European odyssey followed, with the Glasgow side reaching the Round of 32 in the 2012/13 UEFA Women's Champions League.

A spell in England with Notts County saw Leanne play in the first Women's FA Cup final to take place at Wembley, losing to Chelsea in 2015.

SCOTLAND

Leanne won her first Scotland cap as a teenager in 2006. Later, she was part of Scotland's Euro 2017 squad – the first time Scotland Women had qualified for a major tournament – and she also played at the 2019 Women's World Cup before her international retirement in 2021.

INTERNATIONAL BROTHERS

THE SOUTTARS – IF THE CAP FITS

When Rangers' John Souttar scored for Scotland against Iceland in June 2025, he took his international tally up to 2 goals from 16 games. It would surely have been more but for some serious injuries earlier in his career.

He's not the only international central defender in the family. Leicester City's Harry Souttar is his younger but taller sibling, and Harry has notched 11 goals from 36 international appearances, including representing his country at the 2020 Tokyo Olympics and the 2022 FIFA World Cup in Qatar.

Both boys were born and raised in Aberdeen, where their father Jack played for nearby Brechin City. John was first capped for Scotland in 2018, but in 2019 Harry opted to represent Australia, where the boys' mother Heather was born.

The Souttars are not the only football brothers who have chosen different international allegiances.

Can you name the different countries that these sets of brothers have turned out for at international level?

Inaki Williams

Nico Williams

Paul Pogba

Florentin Pogba

Kurt Zouma

Lionel Zouma

Granit Xhaka

Taulant Xhaka

Thiago Alcantra

Rafinha

ANSWERS ON PAGE 60 / 61

COLOURING IN

EUROPEAN NIGHTS

There is nothing like a European night under the lights at Ibrox, although it was mostly Rangers' great form in away games that carried them to the Europa League Quarter Finals in 2025.

A 'home' defeat by Dynamo Kyiv at Hampden Park in August saw Rangers crash out of Champions League qualifying and into the Europa League where they enjoyed eight games in the new expanded group stage format.

Ultimately, the Glasgow giants fell short of repeating their 2022 charge to the Final but the European campaign was a clear highlight of the season and Gers fans enjoyed some unforgettable away trips and several nights of high drama in Govan.

UEFA EUROPA LEAGUE GROUP STAGE

Victory in Malmo on Matchday 1 was Rangers' first ever competitive win in Sweden and got their Europa League adventure off to a good start.

An impressive pyrotechnic display greeted top French side Olympique Lyonnais at Ibrox in October but they quickly stunned the home crowd with doubles from Fofana and Lacazette in an impressive 4-1 win.

A 4-goal win over Romanians FCSB boosted Rangers' goal-difference and that would prove important later, whilst a fine counter-attack goal from Dessers saw the Ibrox men snatch a valuable point from UEFA Conference League champions Olympiacos in Greece.

A trip to Southern France allowed Rangers to cancel out the 4-1 loss to Lyon by defeating Nice by the same score – a performance that thrilled manager Philippe Clement as his team extended their unbeaten away run in Europe under his command to seven games.

Rangers have not defeated English opposition in Europe since a memorable night in Leeds in 1992 and that hoodoo remains after a pair of enthralling "Battle of Britain" games against the two eventual finalists.

Rangers "welcomed" Tottenham Hotspur and former Celtic manager Ange Postecoglou to Ibrox in December. Big Ange's Spurs side secured a draw in Glasgow and would then go on to lift the trophy in Bilbao five months later.

At Old Trafford in January, a stunning late strike by Cyriel Dessers balanced out Jack Butland's early own goal but Bruno Fernandes silenced the celebrations with an even later winner for Amorim's Manchester United.

On Matchday 8, Rangers raced into a 2-0 lead over Belgians USG but had to endure a nervy finish after Kevin Mac Allister was left home alone in the box to loop a header in and cut the deficit. Not only did Rangers hold on, but results elsewhere saw them snatch the eighth and final automatic qualifying spot with the best goal-difference out of the four teams which finished on 14 points.

ROUND OF 16

Rangers 3-3 Fenerbahçe (3-2 penalties)

Barry Ferguson shocked José Mourinho with a surprise change of formation and was rewarded with a stunning 3-1 win in hostile Istanbul. In truth, it could have been more as Cyriel Dessers had two further "goals" ruled out. Mourinho had warned that "it's not over" and he was proved correct when his Fenerbahçe side came to Ibrox. Two unanswered goals over-turned their first leg deficit before Jack Butland's penalty shoot-out saves helped the home side to progress.

QUARTER FINAL

Rangers 0-2 Athletic Bilbao

Rangers were under pressure after Robin Propper was dismissed early in the first leg at Ibrox. A battling performance kept the tie level and it was Liam Kelly's turn to be the penalty hero with a fine late stop.

Barry Ferguson would point to Cyriel Dessers' ripped shirt as evidence that his side should have had a penalty in Bilbao but it was John Souttar who was later penalised. The resulting spot-kick by Sancet and a fine finish by Nico Williams sent the Basques through, but they would not reach the Final at their own San Mames stadium after defeat by Manchester United in the semis.

POSTSCRIPT NOTE

Overall, Rangers' performances on the European stage brought glamour, excitement and pride to the club in an otherwise difficult season. They certainly gave their supporters something to get excited about and probably the club treasurer too!

RANGERS WOMEN: 2024/2025 SEASON REVIEW

"It's déjà vu all over again": Yogi Berra, New York Yankees

For the second season in a row, Jo Potter's Rangers Women went into the final minutes of the league season with a chance of winning a historic treble but, once again and despite a gallant effort, they had to settle for a repeat of last year's cup double.

After coming agonisingly close to delivering back-to-back trebles, Potter moved on to take charge at Crystal Palace in the Summer and left with the best wishes and gratitude of the club.

CHAMPIONS LEAGUE 2024/25

Rangers Women started the season by winning their first five games, scoring 43 goals without conceding any, and went into their UEFA Champions League Round One Qualifying in September 2024 full of confidence. Unfortunately, they then ran into a dominant Arsenal side at Boreham Wood and despite holding the eventual tournament winners to a 1-goal lead at half-time, by full-time the hosts had run up a 6-0 advantage.

Three days later, Rangers again faced formidable opposition – this time, top Spanish Liga F side Atletico Madrid. Once again, the Light Blues came up empty-handed, this time on the wrong side of a 3-0 scoreline which brought their European dream to an end.

SCOTTISH WOMEN'S PREMIER LEAGUE

After 22 games, only three points separated the top four teams at the end of a very competitive SWPL regular season. Rangers sat in 3rd place with a massive +94 goal difference, one point ahead of the previous year's champions, Celtic. A resurgent Glasgow City and a much-improved Hibernian squad topped the table at the split with 54 points apiece to set up a thrilling Championship Round, with the top six teams playing each other home and away to determine the winners.

By the final day of the league season in May, only Hibs and Rangers were still in contention and they faced off at Ibrox with Rangers needing to win to get level on points and take the title, as a result of their massively superior goal difference. Sadly, it was not to be and Linzi Taylor's 74th minute goal for Hibs was enough to clinch a historic triumph for the Leith side. Even worse, Glasgow City's last day win over Hearts secured second place for them and denied Rangers entry into European competition in 2025/26.

HOME

Rangers Women have made a home for themselves at Broadwood Stadium in Cumbernauld but the ladies also enjoy occasional appearances at Ibrox, including a Mother's Day fixture against Hearts in March this year. Pivotal late season fixtures against Glasgow City and Hibs were also played in Govan so that larger crowds could cheer the girls on.

CUP DOUBLE AT THE DOUBLE

Rangers Women dominated knockout competition in Scotland for the second season in a row by repeating their Scottish Cup and League Cup double triumph in 2025.

SKY SPORTS / SWPL CUP FINAL

Hibernian 0-5 Rangers
(Wilkinson, Lafaix, Reilly OG, Howat, Hardy)
Fir Park, Motherwell 22nd March 2025

In front of over 4,000 fans, Rangers swept to victory in the League Cup for the third year in a row with a surprisingly comfortable win over eventual league champions Hibs.

Katie Wilkinson had already scored in each round of the cup run, including a hat-trick against Motherwell, so it was no surprise when she opened the scoring just before half time.

Rangers were in irresistible form and blew the game open with two goals in two minutes just after the breakthrough Camille Lafaix and an own goal from Hibs' Reilly. Kirsty Howat and Rio Hardy added late goals to cap an emphatic team display.

R2	Dundee United	0-3	Rangers
QF	Motherwell	1-8	Rangers
SF	Celtic	1-2	Rangers

SWF SCOTTISH CUP FINAL

Glasgow City 0-3 Rangers
(McAulay, Howat 2)
Hampden Park, Glasgow 25th May 2025

After Rangers cruised through the early rounds, veteran striker Jane Ross stepped up with a Hampden semi-final hat-trick against Aberdeen to send her team through to the Scottish Cup Final. A ten-minute cameo at the end of the final would be Ross' last appearance before retirement but she claimed a winner's medal as Rangers ran out comfortable 3-0 winners.

Katie Wilkinson did not add to her incredible goal-scoring tally but the English woman did play a part in all three goals. After the woodwork denied Rangers twice, Mia McAulay opened the scoring with a precision strike on 25 minutes. Kirsty Howat then took control with a strong turn and finish before half-time and then settled the game by finishing off a fine team move from a Chelsea Cornet assist.

R3	Westdyke Ladies	1-24	Rangers
R4	Rangers	7-0	Montrose
QF	Rangers	2-0	Spatans
SF	Rangers	5-0	Aberdeen

RANGERS WOMEN
LAURA & KATIE

THE RISING STAR

Laura Berry only turned 18-years-old in June 2025 but by then she had already been named PFA Scotland SWPL Young Player of the Year. Laura scored 18 SWPL goals last term in a season split between two stints for Jo Potter's Rangers, either side of a prolific loan spell at Motherwell.

Laura first grabbed the spotlight in 2022 after making her debut for Rangers' first team. She signed her first professional contract at the same time as Mia McAulay in summer 2023.

Having been loaned to Motherwell in 2024, Laura became the youngest ever winner of the SWPL Player of the Month award in April of that year for her performances in claret & amber, and went on to score 11 goals for the Lanarkshire club.

Last season, Laura started the campaign for parent-club Rangers and grabbed attention by notching five goals in five games. A subsequent return to Motherwell on loan saw her score another 11 goals and nab a second SWPL Player of the Month award in September. As a result of these fine achievements, Laura was summoned back to Rangers in January 2025 after signing a new 3-year contract the previous month.

Laura is already part of the Scotland U19 set up and the teenager will be looking forward to making an even bigger name for herself for club and country in the next few years.

HATS OFF TO KATIE

Having turned 30-years old last season, you could almost consider English striker Katie Wilkinson as a veteran, but she was in vintage form throughout her first year in light blue, firing Rangers to cup glory and herself to the top of the scoring charts with a series of prime-time performances.

Katie announced her arrival in the Scottish league with a 4-goal individual blast against Aberdeen in her first competitive game. Nine months later, she topped that with a 5-goal display against Motherwell in May, having scored six hat-tricks in between, including two against the Lanarkshire club.

By the end of the season, Katie had scored 39 individual league goals – that's more than Queen's Park and Dundee United managed as a team in the SWPL.

Unsurprisingly, Katie was Rangers Women's top goal scorer and became the first-ever recipient of the Jane Ross Plate, named in honour of the prolific Rangers & Scotland striker who retired in 2025. Katie also scooped the Players' Player of the Year award and was named to the SWPL Team of the Year.

CHASING THE TITLE DREAM

New manager Leanne Crichton now has the honour of taking the Women's team forward in 2025/26 and will attempt to win back the league title for the first time since season 2021/22.

Despite a few high-profile departures, Leanne has inherited a fine squad of players and there have been some exciting new additions too.

KIRSTY HOWAT #9

Dumfries-born Kirsty won the SWPL Player of the Month award in March after some strong performances and vital goals. A strong finish to the season saw her score twice in the Scottish Cup Final and earn a Scotland recall after being named in new Head Coach Melissa Andreatta's first squad.

LEAH EDDIE #3

Having learned her trade as a footballer at Graeme High School in Falkirk and Central Ladies Academy, Leah Eddie made a name for herself in a six-year stint with Hibernian during which she won her first Scotland caps. The central defender was lured back to Rangers in Summer 2024 and will have particularly enjoyed the Sky Sports Cup victory over her former team.

JENNA FIFE #1

Rangers Women benefitted from the talents of a trio of international goalkeepers last season, but it was Edinburgh veteran Jenna Fife who stood between the sticks for both cup finals and the league-decider. Jenna made her 100th appearance for the club in October 2024 and has now extended her contract until 2028.

ALICE GRIFFITHS #22

The defensive midfielder joined Rangers from Southampton, where she played alongside Katie Wilkinson and Laura Rafferty.

Alice made the switch in Summer 2025 after travelling to the UEFA Women's European Championships with Wales. The 24-year-old from Aberdare has international 16 caps and has signed a 2-year deal.

FALLON CONNOLLY-JACKSON #29

Young Fallon made the switch from Sheffield United in Summer 2025 and will add competition for the full back positions at Ibrox.

The 19-year-old is eligible for Scotland selection through her grandfather and has already appeared at U19 and U23 level.

IBROX STADIUM: 1899-2024
PART 2: THE EVOLUTION OF IBROX

Formed in 1872, Rangers first moved to the burgh of Govan in 1887 (Govan was incorporated into the City of Glasgow in 1912). The original Ibrox Park was built on a site adjacent to the current stadium and served as the club's home from 1887-1899 before being demolished.

What we now know as Ibrox Stadium bears no resemblance to its first incarnation as the "new" Ibrox Park of 1899. The Victorian ground featured an oval track, an ornate pavilion and one grandstand. By 1902, a massive wooden terracing had been added at the western side of the ground, taking capacity to 75,000.

Tragically, 25 supporters were killed when part of the wooden structure collapsed during a Scotland v England match in April 1902. Thereafter, massive slopes were constructed from earth and, after further expansion and the addition of a new Main Stand, a record crowd of 118,567 attended the league match against Celtic on 2nd January 1939.

The magnificent Main Stand was designed by the famed Scottish architect Archibald Leitch and opened on 1st January 1929. Now approaching its own centenary, the iconic red-brick façade makes it one of the most instantly recognisable structures in world football and it is protected as a listed building. Subsequent modernisations have never been allowed to detract from the traditional aesthetic and in 2006 the stand was renamed as the Bill Struth Main Stand in honour of the legendary manager.

The Ibrox Disaster, which saw 66 supporters lose their lives on the notorious Stairway 13 after the Old Firm game on 2nd January 1971, prompted Rangers to rebuild three sides of the ground with new all-seater stands. After construction of the Govan, Broomloan and Copland Road stands, the first match with the current configuration was another Old Firm game on 19th September 1981.

In 2001, thirty years after the 1971 Ibrox Disaster, Rangers unveiled a poignant memorial – a bronze statue of "the greatest ever Ranger" John Greig, created by sculptor Andy Scott, who was also responsible for 'The Kelpies'. The statue is mounted on a large red-brick plinth outside the Main Stand and bears the names of those who lost their lives in the disasters of 1902 and 1971.

WORD SEARCH

We have hidden the names of 10 of Rangers' recent European opponents. Can you find them all?

REAL BETIS   **PANATHINAIKOS**   **ATHLETIC BILBAO**
SPURS   **BENFICA**   **NICE**
MALMO   **FENERBACHE**
LYON   **SPARTA PRAGUE**

ANSWERS ON PAGE 60 / 61

SPOT THE DIFFERENCE

Can you spot the 10 differences between these two photos of the match? Answers on page 61

LEGENDS FEATURE: DAVIE COOPER

On 23rd March 2025, Rangers Football Club paid tribute to the great Davie Cooper on the 30th anniversary of his untimely death, at just 39-years-old.

The legendary winger is still fondly remembered by supporters for his magical left foot, mesmerising dribbling skills and ferocious shot.

Between June 1977 and August 1989, Cooper made over 500 appearances in light blue, collecting 13 winner's medals (3 League, 3 Scottish Cup, 7 Scottish League Cup).

> "God gave Davie Cooper a talent. He would not be disappointed with how it was used."
> **Walter Smith**

> "He was a Brazilian trapped in a Scotsman's body!"
> **Ray Wilkins**

> "He could have played a violin with it."
> **Andy Roxburgh**

COMING TO IBROX

Davie Cooper was born in Hamilton, Lanarkshire. He grew up as a Rangers fan but his playing career started and ended with Clydebank FC. His talent was obvious for all to see, but a starring role against Rangers in the quarter-final of the League Cup in September 1976 made his transfer to Ibrox almost inevitable.

Over the course of four games, Cooper scored the equalizing goal for the under-dogs on three occasions, before Rangers won the second replay to advance.

Nine months later, Jock Wallace cliched his signature after agreeing a fee of £100,000 with the Bankies.

RANGERS' GREATEST EVER GOAL

Cooper had a knack for scoring vital cup final goals but his memorable solo effort against Celtic in the 1979 Drybrough Cup Final at Hampden was his best. Cooper controlled a cross, with his back to goal, before slipping past four Celtic defenders with a series of "keepie-uppies" and slotting home.

In 1999, it was voted by fans as "Rangers' greatest ever goal" and The Guardian once listed it as the "second greatest ever solo goal" behind only Maradona's long dribble against England in 1986.

SCOTLAND

Cooper debuted for Scotland against Peru at Hampden in 1979. He went on to earn 22 caps.

His precision striking ability made him an obvious choice to score the vital penalty on a fateful night in Cardiff that saw Scotland progress in qualification for the 1986 Mexico World Cup. After scoring again in a play-off against Australia, Cooper appeared in two of Scotland's three games in Mexico.

LIFE AFTER RANGERS AND DEATH

Cooper won the league three times, including in his first and last seasons at Ibrox – bridging the nine years between titles before Graeme Souness' arrival in 1986.

Davie also attained legendary status at Motherwell FC after moving there in 1989. Cooper was part of their iconic 4-3 Scottish Cup Final win over Dundee United in 1991 – the Steelmen's first major trophy for 39 years.

After returning to Clydebank as player/coach, Cooper became involved in presenting a coaching series for STV called 'Shoot'. Sadly, while filming an episode in Cumbernauld, he suffered a brain haemorrhage and died on 23rd March 1995.

HIS MEMORY

Davie Cooper is still fondly remembered by those fortunate enough to have seen him in action.

He was inducted into the Rangers Hall of Fame in 2000 and has been similarly honoured at both of his other clubs.

In 1999, a statue was erected in his honour at Hamilton Palace Sports and Recreation Grounds.

The North Stand at Motherwell's Fir Park was renamed "The Davie Cooper Stand".

Ten years after his death, the 2005 Scottish League Cup Final between Rangers and Motherwell is widely known as "The Cooper Final". Tickets for the game featured an image of Cooper and charitable donations were made in his memory.

Supporters of both clubs celebrated his career and the teams, managed by former colleagues Alex McLeish and Terry Butcher, served up a suitably entertaining match, with Rangers romping to a 5-1 victory.

Ibrox has been graced by many fine wingers over the years but there is still only one Davie Cooper.

RANGERS ACADEMY

LOAN RANGERS

In January 2025, Rangers pre-empted changes at national level by effectively disbanding their B Team and focusing on their age group squads. Promising young players like Findlay Curtis and Mason Munn were integrated into the first team squad, while several promising youngsters were sent out on loan to gain practical experience.

Among the loanees, left-back Robbie Fraser starred in Livingston's Championship run-in, featuring in all of their play-off games as the Livi Lions clawed their way back to the Premiership.

Josh Gentles was an instant success at Alloa Athletic, becoming that club's youngest goal scorer for 10 years at the age of 17. The experience helped the Welsh youth international break into Rangers' initial Champions League Squad at the start of this season.

From season 2025/26, clubs may enter into "Co-operation Agreements" with clubs in other divisions regarding player loans. This allows greater flexibility for the players to move freely between the clubs, and is intended to further the progression of Scotland-qualified U21 players.

Northern Irish goalkeeper Mason Munn does not qualify for such an arrangement due to his nationality, but nevertheless joined Neil Lennon's Dunfermline Athletic in the Scottish Championship.

U18s captain Jack Wyllie was loaned to Kelty Hearts in July 2025.

ONE TO WATCH: FINDLAY CURTIS

Young midfielder Findlay Curtis made great strides in 2025. Curtis made his first team debut against Fraserburgh in January 2025. He made his European debut off the bench at Old Trafford a few days later and then signed a contract extension before the month was over.

He would go on to earn his first start at Pittodrie in April 2025 and was promoted to the Scotland U20 squad for the first time in May 2025.

The youngster's progression into the first team continued early this term with an Ibrox goal spree to start the season. Curtis netted against Club Brugge and Middlesborough in pre-season before adding a vital strike against Panathinaikos in the UEFA Champions League.

YOUTH FOCUS: RANGERS U18 / U19

In 2024/25, Rangers finished second in the CAS Elite U18s league, with the title going to Hibs.

The competition will be contested by hybrid U19 teams in 2025/26 with provision for over-age players to participate.

Also in 2025/26, the Challenge Cup has been revamped as the KDM Evolution Trophy, with Premiership U19 teams competing against lower league opposition in an expanded format.

Rangers were drawn against Stenhousemuir, Stranraer, Queen of the South, Annan, Dumbarton and Hamilton, with all of their ties to be played away from home.

GLASGOW CUP DOUBLE WINNERS

Rangers B/U19 side will defend their Glasgow Cup title in 2025/26 having won the competition twice last season!

Firstly, they defeated Celtic 3-2 in December 2024 in the delayed 2023/24 final. Rangers' scorers were Nsio, McKinnon and Lovelace in a side that also featured over-age first teamers Oscar Cortes and Rabbi Matondo.

They followed that up with a penalty shoot-out win over Celtic in the 2024/25 final in April at Firhill Stadium. The match finished 1-1 after a Kasanwirjo goal for Rangers and the young Gers triumphed 5-4 on penalties.

Only Curtis, Nsio and Hutton started both Finals.

AWARDS

On 28th April 2025, the top players from Rangers' men's and women's teams were honoured in a ceremony at The Doubletree Hotel by Hilton in Glasgow. Nico Raskin, Hamza Igamane and Katie Wilkinson were all double-winners on a star-studded night where both squads got the chance to dress up for the occasion.

MEN'S PLAYER OF THE YEAR AND PLAYERS' PLAYER OF THE YEAR:
NICO RASKIN

The young Belgian's industrious performances in midfield were appreciated by both Rangers' supporters and his colleagues. His commitment and willingness to win the ball last season was exceptional and his goals and assists inspired most of the club's best moments.

WOMEN'S PLAYERS' PLAYER OF THE YEAR:
KATIE WILKINSON

Her team-mates had 39 good reasons to pick Katie Wilkinson for this award as that is the number of times the country's top goal-scorer hit the back of the net for Rangers in league matches, scoring three times or more on eight occasions.

WOMEN'S PLAYER OF THE YEAR:
BROGAN HAY

The 26-year-old Glasgow girl has become known for her consistent excellence on the wing and has already won numerous Player of the Month awards in her time with Rangers. The Scotland international has now made over 150 appearances in light blue and continues to set the standard for her team-mates to aspire to.

YOUNG PLAYER OF THE YEAR:
HAMZA IGAMANE AND MIA MCAULAY

Moroccan Hamza Igamane showed great appetite and potential in his first season in Scotland. He grabbed attention with some fine European performances, including a brace away to Nice, while a hat-trick at Hibernian in January 2025 helped earn him SPL Player of the Month honours.

Mia McAulay continued her rise in the Women's game with some eye-catching performances. A typical precision strike opened the scoring in the season-ending Scottish Women's Cup Final at Hampden in May and there was more joy for Mia later that month when she appeared for Scotland for the first time.

NIGHT 2025

JOHN GREIG CBE ACHIEVEMENT AWARD:
JOHN SOUTTAR

This award is made in recognition of commitment and dedication to the club, and the greatest-ever-Ranger chose consistent defender John Souttar for the honour this year. In his third season at Ibrox, Souttar made 40 appearances and was again a rock at the heart of the Rangers defence. His performances were also appreciated outside the club as he was a regular for Scotland and was also elected to the PFA Scotland Team of the Year.

JANE ROSS PLATE:
KATIE WILKINSON

For the first time, the award for Women's Top Goal Scorer was named in honour of retiring legend Jane Ross. The 35-year-old has performed at a high level over 19 years, including 151 caps and 62 goals for Scotland. The day before the awards, Jane hit a hat-trick for Rangers in the Scottish Cup semi-final against Aberdeen in a season when she also netted five times in a game against Dundee United. Katie Wilkinson was the inaugural winner for her phenomenal goal-scoring record in 2024/25.

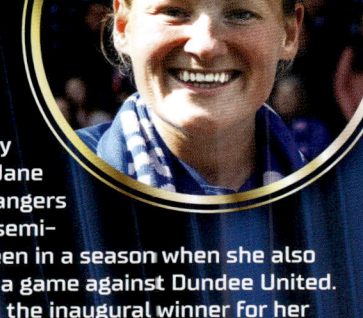

ACADEMY PLAYER OF THE YEAR:
AIDEN McCALLION

The young red-headed midfielder only turned 17 years old in June 2025 but he has already been part of the Rangers First Team squad, including the trip to Bilbao.

Despite his youth and inexperience, it was Aiden who stepped up to score the decisive penalty for Rangers in a sudden-death shoot-out win over Celtic in the Glasgow Cup Final this year.

SAM ENGLISH BOWL:
CYRIEL DESSERS

Like Wilkinson, Dessers was the top-scorer in the league and now has over 100 appearances and 50 goals in Rangers' colours. His goal at Old Trafford was a highlight and immediately after the end of the domestic season, he kept on scoring at international level for Nigeria.

500 APPEARANCES RECOGNITION:
JAMES TAVERNIER

After 10 years at Ibrox, during which time he has won all three major domestic competitions, established himself as the highest-scoring defender in UK football history and captained the side through good times and bad; James Tavernier made his 500th appearance for Rangers on 1st March 2025. He then scored his 130th goal for the club shortly after – a remarkable record of loyalty and distinction which was rightly recognised by a special award on the night.

IBROX STADIUM: 1899-2024
PART 3: MODERN IBROX

Ibrox is constantly evolving to keep pace with innovation, generate revenue and provide the best possible fan experience.

The Govan Stand has been augmented with the Argyle House extension and now boasts additional executive boxes and hospitality areas, including Bar 72, which commemorates the Rangers team which won the European Cup Winners Cup in 1972. The stand was re-named in honour of one of the legendary stars of that team, Sandy Jardine, in 2014.

In 2024, a statue of former manager Walter Smith was unveiled in front of the Copland Road Stand.

Maximum attendance has been increased in several ways. A third tier was added to the Main Stand in 1991 to accommodate the new Club Deck. Reconfiguring passageways and lowering the pitch all facilitated increased seating and both corners of the Govan Stand were filled in with seating and giant screens. By 2025, capacity had increased to 51,700.

The most recent developments at the stadium have focused on improving the experience for supporters with disabilities. The creation of raised platforms in the heart of "the Rangers End" has improved the viewing experience and this has been augmented by lifts, lowered kiosks and accessible toilets.

In addition, the club has created Broxi's Den – a neurodiverse sensory room for fans with conditions such as autism and ADHD. The club also has provision for blind and deaf supporters and offers bespoke support for other conditions through its Disability Matters group.

Of course, what happens on the pitch is still of primary importance, as is the pitch itself. In May 2025, Rangers were presented with the inaugural SPFL Pitch of the Season Award.

HOW WELL DO YOU KNOW OLIVER ANTMAN?

Oliver Antman signed for Rangers from Dutch side Go Ahead Eagles in August 2025.

The 24-year-old Finnish winger joined the Eredivisie club in August 2024. In his only season with them, he scored six goals in 32 appearances, plus a league-leading 15 assists, while helping the Eagles to win the KNVB Cup for the first time.

With Rangers, Oliver will be hoping to add to his tally of 22 international caps. So far, he has scored seven international goals, including one against Scotland at Hampden Park in June 2024.

How well do you know Oliver Antman? Answer these questions to test your Antman knowledge.

1. Which city in the Netherlands are Go Ahead Eagles from?

2. Oliver played for Danish Superliga club FC Nordsjælland alongside which current Rangers team-mate?

3. On 26th December 2022 in Podgorica, Oliver scored on his international debut against which Balkan nation?

4. Who played the title role in the 2015 Marvel movie Ant Man?

ANSWERS ON PAGE 60 / 61

GETTING TO KNOW: DJEIDI GASSAMA

CHILDHOOD

Djeidi Hamara Gassama was born on 10th September 2003 in the village of Niéléba Haouissé in the Saharan country of Mauritania – a small, former French colony in North West Africa with a population of just over 4 million.

After moving to France as a child, Djeidi began to make a name for himself at the youth academies of Brest (Belgium) and Paris Saint-Germain.

PARIS SAINT-GERMAIN

Djeidi made his only appearance for the PSG first team as an 18-year-old in May 2022. He replaced Argentinian Angel Di Maria in the 88th minute of the French champions' 4-0 victory over Montpellier and enjoyed a few minutes on the pitch up front with Lionel Messi and Kylian Mbappe.

K.A.S. EUPEN

In September 2022, Djeidi moved to K.A.S. Eupen on a season-long loan.

The Qatari-owned East Belgian club played in the second tier Challenger Pro League and Djeidi scored twice in 18 appearances for the Pandas.

Djeidi also made his first appearances for France U20s in September 2022.

SHEFFIELD WEDNESDAY

Djeidi moved from Paris to Yorkshire for season 2023/24 and immediately showed flashes of potential for Wednesday.

Now in his 20s, Djeidi really hit his stride in his second season at Hillsborough, scoring 8 goals from 43 games and also becoming one of the most fouled players in the Championship.

The young man was voted as Player of the Year by one veteran supporters' group and Owls fans were very disappointed to see him move to Rangers in 2025 for a bargain fee as a financial squeeze affected the cash-strapped Sheffield club.

FAST START

Apparently, Djeidi turned up to a hastily-arranged first meeting with Rangers officials while wearing the training gear of the NBA basketball club Boston Celtics. Oops!

After signing, Djeidi made a much better first impression on Rangers fans, becoming an instant hero with his vital goals in the UEFA Champions League qualifiers.

SPOT THE BALL

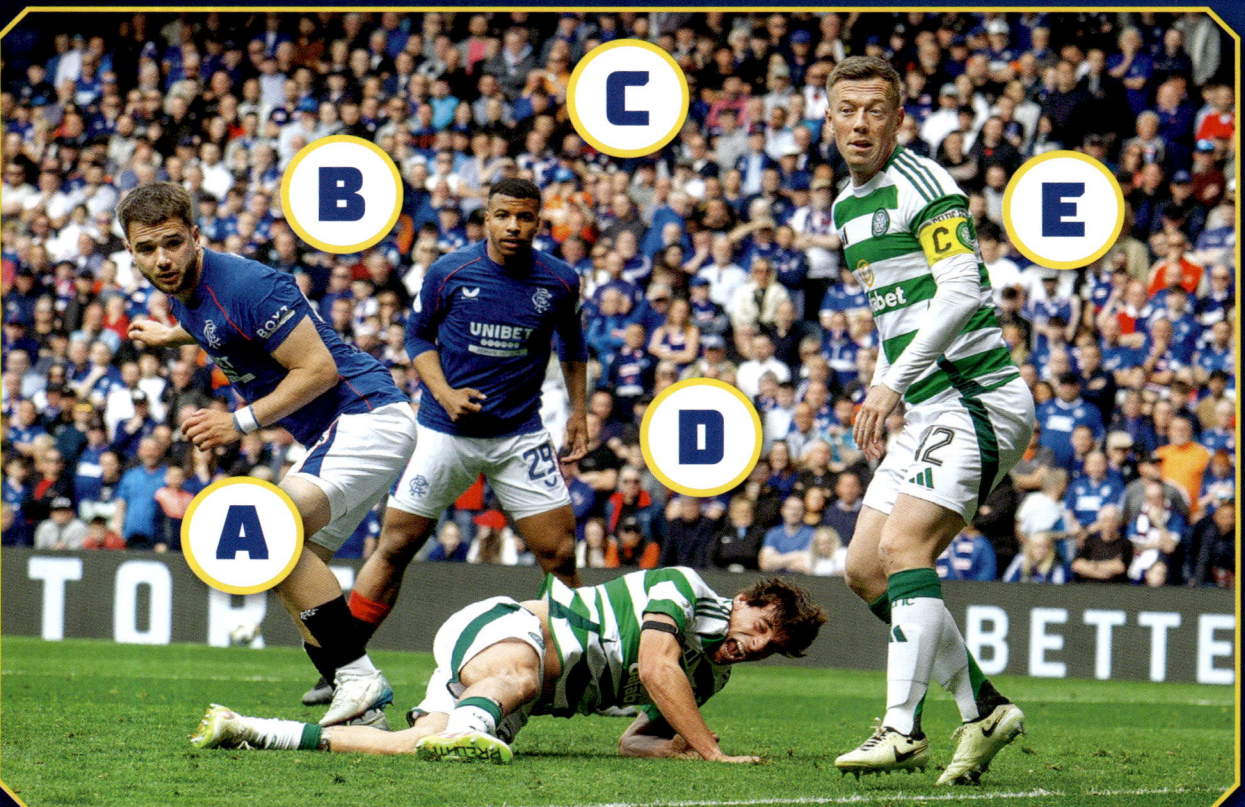

ANAGRAMS

Can you unscramble the following anagrams to identify the names of ten Ibrox favourites; 1 Manager, 7 Men's team players and 2 from the Women's team.

DIAMOND HOMEMADE

ARREST MULLINS

CAROLINA SKINS

ASSIGNED JAR

AGATHA RELOADS

HOLLOWER JET

SHOUT TROJAN

CLARIFY NUDIST

ADELE HIDE

HANKY THRILL

ANSWERS ON PAGES 61

WHO ARE THE SAN FRANCISCO 49ERS?

After a multi-million-pound transaction last summer, majority ownership of Rangers was bought by a consortium headed jointly by US healthcare tycoon Andrew Cavenagh and 49ers Enterprises (the corporate investment arm of the San Francisco 49ers NFL team).

Here are some interesting facts about the 49ers.

HISTORY

The team first played in 1946 and were named in reference to the "Miner 49ers" – prospectors from the California gold rush of 1849.

LEVI'S STADIUM

In 2014, the team moved to a new state-of-the-art stadium in Santa Clara, approximately 40 miles south of the city of San Francisco.

With a capacity of around 70,000, the stadium has previously hosted WrestleMania, music concerts, and even an outdoor NHL ice hockey game.

Levi's Stadium is due to host the Super Bowl for a second time in February 2026. Later in the year, it will also be the venue for six games in the 2026 FIFA World Cup.

SUPER BOWLS

So far, the team has enjoyed five Super Bowl winning seasons; 1981, 1984, 1988, 1989, 1994.

The 1980s were a golden period for the team. Led by Head Coach Bill Walsh and legendary quarterback Joe Montana, a win over Cincinnati in Super Bowl XVI kick-started a dynastic decade. Newer stars like Steve Young and Jerry Rice helped deliver back-to-back wins starting in 1988 and a record-breaking 5th win in 14 years in 1994.

THE CAPTAIN: NICOLA DOCHERTY

Nicola Docherty knows all about winning – after all, she grew up as a life-long Rangers supporter, attending games as a young girl with her Father Nicky.

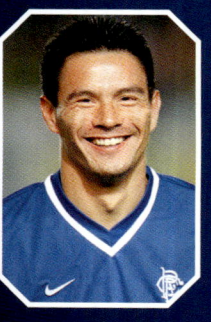

Falkirk lass Nicola once named Michael Mols as her first Rangers hero – the Dutch striker was part of two league-winning sides at Ibrox, either side of the turn of the century – but her own talents lie on the left side of the defence.

As a 33- year-old woman, Nicola has achieved what her younger self probably couldn't even have dreamt of at that time – life as a full-time professional footballer, 63 caps for Scotland, and over 100 games as captain of Rangers, including being the first player to get her hands on both domestic cups in each of the last two years.

Through it all, she is still a Rangers fan – travelling to Seville with two of her team mates to see the Men's team go for glory in the Europa League Final in Seville in 2022, completing the last leg of the journey by supporters' club bus.

Having started her career with Falkirk and Rangers, Nicola went on to win an incredible 17 medals over eight years as a player with Glasgow City, including eight consecutive league titles.

Nicola returned to Rangers in 2020 as the Women's team went full-time, helping to win the league in 2021/22 and taking over as captain in 2024.

Nicola's Scotland career began in 2011 and includes appearances against England and Argentina in the 2019 Women's World Cup. Of her two international goals, the only goal of the game in a win over Australia at Wimbledon, England is probably the highlight.

Having participated in a period of unprecedented growth in the Women's game, the now-veteran Docherty has still got a lot to contribute through her contributions both on and off the pitch.

Rangers and her team-mates are fortunate to have her.

IBROX STADIUM: 1899-2024
PART 4: FAMOUS IBROX MOMENTS

Ibrox has been host to some fabulous moments over the years – and not all of them football related!

A VISIT FROM THE KING

King George V and Queen Mary visited Ibrox on 17th September 1917 to thank the people of Glasgow and Clydeside for their efforts in the First World War.

In 1938, King George VI made a live broadcast to the nation from Ibrox during the opening ceremony for the Empire Exhibition – widely believed to be the basis for the film 'The King's Speech'.

NOVEMBER 1945 RANGERS 2 DYNAMO MOSCOW 2

Just a few months after the end of the Second World War, Soviet side Dynamo Moscow undertook a short British tour. Remarkably, over 90,000 crammed into Ibrox to see them, even though the match took place at 2:15 on a Wednesday afternoon.

Rangers wore a change strip of thin blue and white hoops to avoid a clash and scored the last two goals to salvage a draw in a memorable fixture.

The sides would meet again in the 1972 European Cup Winners' Cup Final.

1972 EUROPEAN CUP WINNERS' CUP SEMI-FINAL 2ND LEG

RANGERS 2 BAYERN MUNICH 0 (AGG 3-1)

A crowd in excess of 80,000 welcomed German World Cup stars like Maier, Beckenbauer, Breitner and Muller to Ibrox after a 1-1 first-leg draw in Munich.

Sandy Jardine scored in the first minute and a second goal from 18-year-old Derek Parlane clinched the tie to set up a trip to Barcelona for the final, which Rangers won to claim their first European trophy.

CONCERTS

Famous musicians who have performed at Ibrox include Frank Sinatra, Rod Stewart, Elton John and Billy Joel. Bon Jovi notched a hat-trick between 1996 and 2007 and, more recently, Harry Styles appeared in 2022.

PREMIER LEAGUE DECIDER 11 MAY 1991

RANGERS 2 ABERDEEN 0

The 1990/91 season reached a dramatic finale with a last day decider at Ibrox. Aberdeen travelled to Glasgow needing only a draw to clinch the title as both sides were locked on 53 points but with the Dons holding a 2-goal advantage.

A patched-up Rangers side featuring tough guys like Terry Hurlock, John Brown and Ian Ferguson took the fight on in front of a raucous Govan crowd. Powerful striker Mark Hateley was the hero of the day with both goals in a 2-0 win as Rangers clinched their third title in a row, in what would eventually become nine-in-a-row.

Remarkably, this was only Walter Smith's fourth game in charge following Graeme Souness' abrupt departure, and he later described the win as the greatest of his time in charge.

OTHER SPORTS

In June 1980, Scottish boxer Jim Watt defended his WBC Lightweight title against American Howard Davis at Ibrox. Around 15,000 fans attended on a wet Glasgow night.

Ibrox also hosted the Rugby Sevens event at the 2014 Commonwealth Games. Over 171,000 fans attended over the course of two days. South Africa beat New Zealand in the final.

A LOOK BACK IN TIME

Rangers will be going for glory again in the 2025/26 season.

The Ibrox club have won many honours over their long history, but inevitably some years are better than others.

In this feature, we look back in time to previous seasons and remember some of the highs and lows.

5 YEARS AGO 2020/21: LEAGUE TITLE #55

After nine barren years, Rangers finally won their elusive 55th Scottish top-league title in 2021. Rivals Celtic had won every flag during the intervening nine years, but in early March, their failure to win at Tannadice handed the title to the Gers and sparked wild scenes as crowds gathered at Ibrox to celebrate.

Rangers eventually finished unbeaten in the league with 102 points; 25 points more than Celtic in 2nd place. Rangers also won all 19 home league games at Ibrox. A superb season-long defensive display resulted in a record-equalling 26 clean sheets and Rangers also set a new British record by conceding only 13 goals in their 32 wins and six draws.

Unsurprisingly, Steven Gerrard was honoured as Manager of the Year by both the PFA and SPFL. 3 different Rangers players were honoured by national bodies as Player of the Year: Steven Davis (SFWA), goalie Allan McGregor (SPFL) and overall top-scorer James Tavernier (PFA Scotland).

10 YEARS AGO 2015/16: THE GOOD, THE BAD AND THE UGLY

Despite another season disfigured by serious legal and financial issues, Rangers completed their journey back to Scotland's top division by winning the SPFL Championship ahead of Falkirk and Hibs.

With the help of manager Mark Warburton's "magic hat", Rangers also won the Challenge Cup and defeated rivals Celtic in a semi-final penalty shoot-out to reach the Scottish Cup Final. After a pulsating final, Rangers slipped to a 3-2 defeat as Hibs lifted the cup for the first time since 1902. There were some ugly scenes after the final whistle as fans clashed on the pitch.

Three Rangers players topped 50 appearances; goalkeeper Wes Foderingham, James Tavernier, and captain Lee Wallace, who was named Championship Player of the Year.

30 YEARS AGO 1995/96: EIGHT-IN-A-ROW

This was the season that Paul Gascoigne arrived at Ibrox to help Rangers win their 8th consecutive title. Other new faces included Gordan Petric and Derek McInnes, in addition to a core of Goram, Gough, McCall, Laudrup, Durie and McCoist.

Rangers made it a double with a 5-1 thumping of Hearts in the Scottish Cup Final and Gazza waltzed off with Player of the Year honours.

50 YEARS AGO 1975/76

Manager Jock Wallace roared Rangers on to their 3rd domestic treble, clinching the first ever Scottish Premier Division title ahead of Celtic and Hibs.

First, Rangers won the League Cup in October 1975, defeating Celtic with the only goal – a flying header by Alex MacDonald. MacDonald also scored in the 3-1 victory over Hearts in the Scottish Cup Final. Derek Johnstone scored the other two and the big man finished with 31 goals for the season as captain John Greig lifted all three major trophies.

SQUAD PROFILES NEW SIGNINGS

MAX AARONS #3

DoB 4 January 2000
Country England (Jamaican qualified)
Position Right Back
Previous Club Bournemouth (on loan)

The exciting full-back arrived at Ibrox in June 2025 via a zig-zagging career journey.

At the age of 14, Max fell out of organized football for two years. After signing for Norwich City, he worked under Matt Gill in the U23 side and trained alongside current boss Russell Martin. He made over 200 first team appearances for the Canaries before joining Bournemouth in 2023, shortly after winning the UEFA U21 Championship with England.

A loan spell at Valencia from January 2025 yielded only four appearances, but that included two games against Barcelona and an away win at Real Madrid.

JOE ROTHWELL #6

DoB 11/01/1995
Country England
Position Midfielder
Previous Club AFC Bournemouth

The experienced play-maker had one of the best passing accuracy ratings in the English Championship and brings a calm head to Rangers' midfield.

The former Manchester United academy player initially made his name with Oxford United in League One before a successful spell in the Championship with Blackburn Rovers. He then played for AFC Bournemouth in the EPL before turning into a Championship promotion specialist – helping both Russell Martin's Southampton and then Leeds United gain promotion to the English Premier League in the last two seasons, while on loan.

Although born in Manchester, Rothwell could be eligible to play for Scotland through his granny.

LYALL CAMERON #16

DoB 10 October 2002
Country Scotland
Position Midfielder
Previous Club Dundee

An attacking midfielder, Lyall debuted for his home-town club Dundee at the age of 16 and went on to make 119 appearances and score 33 goals for the Dens Park men.

Even after signing a pre-contract agreement with Rangers in January 2025, Lyall performed some late season heroics to help preserve Dundee's top league status, including two vital goals on the final day.

Cameron has 12 Scotland U21 caps and will be expected to provide plenty of goals and assists in a Rangers shirt.

EMMANUEL FERNANDEZ #37

DoB 20/11/2001
Country England
Position Central Defender
Previous Club Peterborough United

Emmanuel Fernandez can include Gillingham, Sheppey United, Margate, Ramsgate, Spalding United and Barnet among his former clubs after a series of loans and permanent moves.

Still only 23 years old, he made his name with Peterborough United, helping them win the 2025 EFL Trophy Final at Wembley against a Birmingham City team featuring Ben Davies and Kieran Dowell.

The tall defender joined Rangers in July 2025 and will continue to wear number 37 in tribute to his brother who was that age when he died.

THELO AASGAARD #11

DoB 02/05/2002
Country Norway
Position Midfielder
Previous Club Luton Town

Thelo Aasgaard was born in Liverpool, England and is eligible to play for France through his mother, but he has chosen to represent his father's country, Norway, at international level. He made his debut in a World Cup qualifier in Moldova in March 2025 and claimed a goal and an assist.

Thelo earned his cap through some fine performances for Luton Town in the Championship after signing for them in January 2025. The Hatters second relegation at the end of the season opened the door for Rangers to swoop and bring the exciting midfielder to Scotland.

Aasgaard initially came through the youth ranks at Liverpool, but really made a name for himself after switching to Blackburn Rovers and breaking into the first team there.

NASSER DJIGA #24

DoB 15/11/2002
Country Burkina Faso
Position Defender
Previous Club Wolverhampton (on loan)

Standing tall at 6 ft 4 inches, Nasser signed for Wolves in 2025 and made 5 appearances for the EPL side last season. Following his season-long loan to Rangers, he immediately slotted in beside John Souttar in defence as Rangers started their Champions League campaign.

The Burkina Faso international first moved to Europe in 2021 to play for Basel in Switzerland. He also gained additional experience on loan to Nimes in France. A move to FK Crvena Zvezda (Red Star Belgrade) resulted in a Serbian league and cup double and helped earn his high-profile move to the Midlands.

DJEIDI GASSAMA #23

DoB 10/09/2003
Country Mauritania (France)
Position Winger
Previous Club Sheffield Wednesday

The flying winger got off to a great start at Ibrox with his goals against Panathinaikos helping Rangers to advance in Europe.

A bargain buy at just over £2m from crisis-club Sheffield Wednesday, the youngster had already made a big impression in the English Championship and had even appeared alongside Messi and Mbappe for PSG while still a teenager.

Although born in Africa, Gassama has already represented France at U20 level and can expect to showcase his talent on the European stage with the Gers.

OLIVER ANTMAN #18

DoB 15/08/2001
Country Finland
Position Winger
Previous Club Go Ahead Eagles

Although only 24 years old, the Finnish star has already experienced football at home and at the top level in Denmark and the Netherlands.

The young man has already developed a reputation as an assist king and will look to add goals to his resume while developing his career in Scotland.

Like his new team-mate Djeidi Gassama, Oliver endeared himself to the Ibrox faithful with a sparkling Champions League debut, which inevitably resulted in an assist.

MIKEY MOORE #47

DoB 11/08/2007
Country England
Position Winger
Previous Club Tottenham Hotspur (on loan)

Although still only 18 years old, Mikey Moore has been playing above his age group for years.

In May 2024, he became Tottenham's youngest ever Premier League debutant when he came on against Manchester City in London.

Mikey's only senior goal for Spurs came in a UEFA Europa League match against IF Elfsborg in January 2025. At only 17 years and 172 days old, his goal broke Jimmy Greaves' record as England's youngest-ever scorer in European competition which had stood since 1957.

Moore was an unused sub in last season's Europa League Final and did not feature against Rangers in the Group phase, although his mentor Jermaine Defoe, a former Ranger, told him what to expect at Ibrox and recommended taking up the option of a loan move to Govan.

Mikey has made a string of appearances for England age-group sides and featured in this summer's UEFA European U19 Championship.

BOJAN MIOVSKI #28

DoB 24/06/1999
Country North Macedonia
Position Striker
Previous Club Girona

Prolific goal-scorer Miovski made a surprise return to Scotland in August 2025, signing from La Liga side Girona for a bargain fee and then going straight into the line-up against Celtic for the first Old Firm derby of the season.

The prolific North Macedonian is known to Rangers supporters from a two-year spell with Aberdeen, where he bagged 44 goals for the Dons between 2022 and 2024. He was named in the PFA Scotland Team of the Year for 2023-24 before his move to Spain in August 2024 which netted a club record fee of £6.8m for the Pittodrie side.

IBROX STADIUM: 1899-2024
PART 5: INSIDE IBROX

The finest traditions of the club are preserved and respected in the most celebrated areas within the majestic and elegant Bill Struth Main Stand at Ibrox.

THE MARBLE STAIRCASE

The sweeping marble staircase at Ibrox is one of the finest entrances of any football stand in the land. Adorned with historic portraits, busts and honours boards, the staircase sets a suitably noble tone for any visit to Ibrox.

THE MANAGER'S OFFICE

The perfectly preserved historical office is a fitting memorial to the man after whom the Main Stand is named.

THE BLUE ROOM

This grand old room is used by the directors of the club on match days and is also the site of most major announcements.

The wooden panelling is believed to be that used for the Clyde-built RMS Queen Mary and elegant portraits and murals adorn the walls, which also feature a marble fireplace.

TROPHY ROOM

As one of the most decorated clubs in the world, Rangers are only able to exhibit a selection of their honours, alongside other historical artefacts and gifts from visiting clubs.

HOME DRESSING ROOM

Rangers players cannot fail to grasp the stature of the club while preparing for action. A portrait of the reigning monarch always looks down from the wooden walls and the club crest is proudly displayed on the floor.

ANSWERS

P24 INTERNATIONAL BROTHERS

Inaki Williams (Ghana)

Nico Williams (Spain)

Paul Pogba (France)

Florentin Pogba (Guinea)

Kurt Zouma (France)

Lionel Zouma (Central African Republic)

Granit Xhaka (Switzerland)

Taulant Xhaka (Albania)

Thiago Alcantara (Spain)

Rafinha (Brazil)

P34 WORD SEARCH

P35 SPOT THE DIFFERENCE

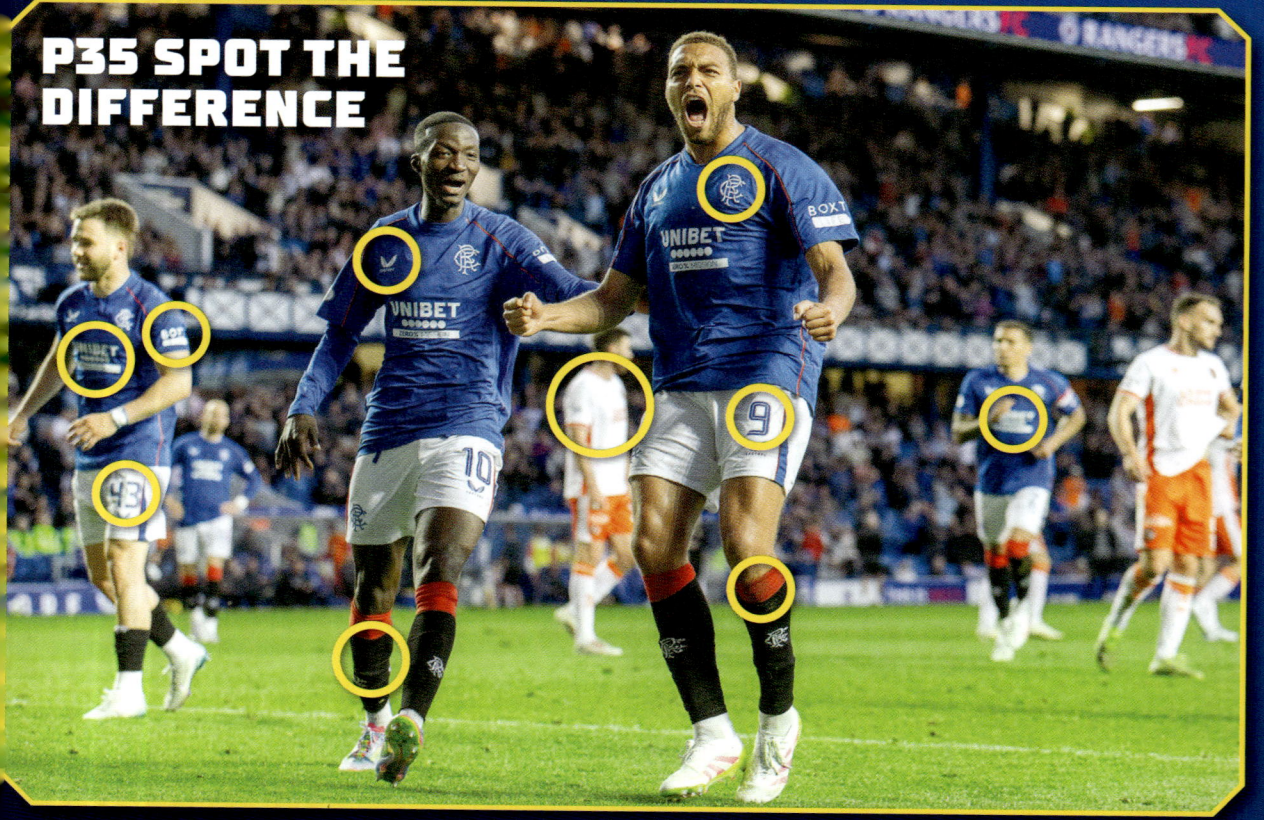

P44 HOW WELL DO YOU KNOW OLIVER ANTMAN?

1. Deventer   2. Mohamed Diomande   3. Montenegro   4. Paul Rudd

P46 SPOT THE BALL   Answer: C

ANAGRAMS

DIAMOND HOMEMADE	Mohamed Diomande
ARREST MULLINS	Russell Martin
CAROLINA SKINS	Nicolas Raskin
ASSIGNED JAR	Nasser Djiga
AGATHA RELOADS	Thelo Aasgard
HOLLOWER JET	Joe Rothwell
SHOUT TROJAN	John Souttar
CLARIFY NUDIST	Findlay Curtis
ADELE HIDE	Leah Eddie
HANKY THRILL	Kathryn Hill

CLUB HONOURS

EUROPEAN CUP WINNERS' CUP
1971-72

SCOTTISH PREMIERSHIP
1890-91, 1898-99, 1899-1900, 1900-01, 1901-02, 1910-11, 1911-12, 1912-13, 1917-18, 1919-20, 1920-21, 1922-23, 1923-24, 1924-25, 1926-27, 1927-28, 1928-29, 1929-30, 1930-31, 1932-33, 1933-34, 1934-35, 1936-37, 1938-39, 1946-47, 1948-49, 1949-50, 1952-53, 1955-56, 1956-57, 1958-59, 1960-61, 1962-63, 1963-64, 1974-75, 1975-76, 1977-78, 1986-87, 1988-89, 1989-90, 1990-91, 1991-92, 1992-93, 1993-94, 1994-95, 1995-96, 1996-97, 1998-99, 1999-2000, 2002-03, 2004-05, 2008-09, 2009-10, 2010-11, 2020-21

SCOTTISH CHAMPIONSHIP
2015-16

SCOTTISH LEAGUE ONE
2013-14

SCOTTISH LEAGUE TWO
2012-13

SCOTTISH CUP
1893-94, 1896-97, 1897-98, 1902-03, 1927-28, 1929-30, 1931-32, 1933-34, 1934-35, 1935-36, 1947-48, 1948-49, 1949-50, 1952-53, 1959-60, 1961-62, 1962-63, 1963-64, 1965-66, 1972-73, 1975-76, 1977-78, 1978-79, 1980-81, 1991-92, 1992-93, 1995-96, 1998-99, 1999-2000, 2001-02, 2002-03, 2007-08, 2008-09, 2021-22

SCOTTISH LEAGUE CUP
1946-47, 1948-49, 1960-61, 1961-62, 1963-64, 1964-65, 1970-71, 1975-76, 1977-78, 1978-79, 1981-82, 1983-84, 1984-85, 1986-87, 1987-88, 1988-89, 1990-91, 1992-93, 1993-94, 1996-97, 1998-99, 2001-02, 2002-03, 2004-05, 2007-08, 2009-10, 2010-11, 2023-24

SCOTTISH CHALLENGE CUP
2015-16

EMERGENCY WAR LEAGUE
1939-40

EMERGENCY WAR CUP
1939-40

SOUTHERN LEAGUE
1940-41, 1941-42, 1942-43, 1943-44, 1944-45, 1945-46

SOUTHERN LEAGUE CUP
1940-41, 1941-42, 1942-43, 1944-45

GLASGOW LEAGUE
1895-96, 1897-98

GLASGOW CUP
1893, 1894, 1897, 1898, 1900, 1901, 1902, 1911, 1912, 1913, 1914, 1918, 1919, 1922, 1923, 1924, 1925, 1930, 1932, 1933, 1934, 1936, 1937, 1938, 1940, 1942, 1943, 1944, 1945, 1948, 1950, 1954, 1957, 1958, 1960, 1969, 1971, 1975 (shared), 1976, 1979, 1983, 1985, 1986, 1987

VICTORY CUP
1946

SUMMER CUP
1942

GLASGOW MERCHANTS CHARITY CUP
1878-79, 1896-97, 1899-1900, 1903-04, 1905-06, 1906-07, 1908-09, 1910-11, 1918-19, 1921-22, 1922-23, 1924-25, 1927-28, 1928-29, 1929-30, 1930-31, 1931-32, 1932-33, 1933-34, 1938-39, 1939-40, 1940-41, 1941-42, 1943-44, 1944-45, 1945-46, 1946-47, 1947-48, 1950-51, 1954-55, 1956-57, 1959-60